Winning Spirit Business

Sharpen Your Performance Edge

Tom Mitchell, Ph.D.

Hilleary Hoskinson

Dedicated to our friends and clients who have shared their professional journeys with us.

CONTENTS

Section 3: The Mental Edge

Section 4: Connections

Section 5: Comeback

Section 6: Post Game

Tom Mitchell

Many years ago, I wrote a book to help my daughters mentally prepare for their athletic and artistic performances. They had fallen in love with ballet and competitive ice-skating, two endeavors I knew little about. However, I wanted to help them tap into their inner game and develop an advantage, a mental edge.

Since then, I have co-authored *Winning Spirit: 16 Timeless Principles That Drive Performance Excellence*, with NFL legend Joe Montana and *Winning Spirit Basketball* with NBA Hall of Famer Chris Mullin, both focusing on both personal and performance growth.

Joe, Hilleary, and I founded MVP Performance Institute, knowing that regardless of the business or industry, leaders of companies are always looking for ways to improve their own "game" and "team."

We have found that when our clients apply the philosophies and practices in this book, they experience very powerful and positive outcomes. We are confident you, too, will see great results as you apply the *winning spirit* to your business life.

Hilleary Hoskinson

I deeply appreciate Tom collaborating with me on this book. I first met him when he was assigned to be my executive coach. I was a senior leader in an internet company with a challenging culture. He coached me through some very turbulent times. His direct and honest feedback always had my best interest at heart. He pushed me to play to my strengths and own my weaknesses. Consciously working on my performance edge activated my professional power in ways I could not have imagined at the time.

Years later, Tom and I, along with Joe Montana, formed our company, MVP Performance Institute. Tom had written a book called *Finding Greatness Within Ice Skating,* for his daughters. Those forty, plain spoken truths became the fundamentals of our company.

Since forming MVP almost a decade ago, I have become even more committed to our principles and methods because our clients get results. Our work requires self-reflection, courage, and practice. Basic? Yes. Effective? Yes. Easy? Not always. Worth it? You bet!

Our Thanks To . . .

Charles Darr, who served as our editorial and design
consultant for this project.

Sean Donovan, who designed and executed the
illustrations in this book. His infinite patience,
skilled hand, and willing imagination helped us
bring abstract concepts into visual expression.

Zach Heffner, of Verdict Digital, who edited all the
photo images in the book. His keen eye and
artful treatment of each photo gives visual
focus to each chapter's theme.

How to Use this Book

Winning Spirit Business is written to help bring the best out of you. While some of the practices encourage you to enlist help from a teammate, a boss, or a coach, this is mostly private work.

This book is not designed to be read from beginning to end. You will have to create your own path. The best way to start is to go online to *www.mvpperformance.com* and take *The Winning Spirit Business Online Assessment.* Your individual results will help you to identify the sections or chapters that might have the greatest initial impact for you.

There are also blank pages at the ends of all chapters upon which you could track your practice. These pages could also be used to remake the book into a journal of your personal insights. Work in the areas where you see the greatest opportunity for growth and change. Use this book as a tool to improve your performance edge.

Most of all, enjoy the journey!

www.mvpperformance.com

Section 1
The Basics

The basics cover self-reflection: identifying personal strengths and weaknesses, developing listening skills, setting expectations, becoming aware of an "inner coach," journaling, and giving and receiving feedback.

2

1

The Power of the Pen

You are the most important project

It is a good practice to keep a private journal of your progress. It will help you become clearer about what you want to accomplish in business and in your personal life. You may find that writing down your thoughts increases your motivation and confidence. Writing often makes things more "real." Your desire and emotion are right there on the page, and the power of your own words can inspire you.

Writing helps you to clarify and focus your thoughts and to keep track of your progress. In your journal, we encourage you to capture your: strengths and weaknesses; ideas and visions; successes and challenges; and observations about things that worked and those that did not. These real life experiences shape your beliefs as a leader and performer. Remember, you are worth writing about.

PRACTICE

Invest in a journal that you will enjoy using frequently. Many of our chapters have practices that ask you to self-reflect and write things down. We have found that writing about your aspirations helps to clarify and prioritize what you really want. Reflecting on your achievements, successes, and challenges accelerates your journey to greater self-awareness.

Make writing a regular practice. If you want to experience change more quickly, track your progress frequently. Journaling will keep your goals within reach and will inspire you to focus with greater intensity.

Every now and then, it is a good idea to re-read the things you have written. You may be pleasantly surprised by your personal development. It also reminds you of issues you still need to address.

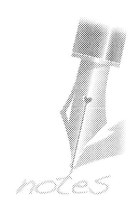

2

The Value of Self-reflection

Play to your strengths

It is important to evaluate yourself as a leader and performer. Asking honest questions about your skills and behaviors will help clarify where you stand. You will discover your strengths and weaknesses and have a better understanding of how you are improving.

Identifying your strengths will build your confidence. Don't undervalue them. Playing to your strengths is your most direct path to success. By identifying your weaknesses, you can focus on improvement. A weakness that you are not aware of is a blind spot. Failure to recognize it can be damaging to your career. The truth is we all have blind spots and we must have the courage to discover what they are.

PRACTICE

In your journal, make a list of every one of your strengths relating to your work. Include both your technical skills as well as intangibles of leadership, communication, and teamwork. Do the same for your weaknesses. Then go back through the lists, and put a plus [+] if you think you are good, and double plus [++] if you are very good. Do the same with your weaknesses using minus [-] and double minus [--]. Be completely honest with yourself.

Don't hold back. Knowing your strengths and weaknesses creates greater personal power and self-awareness.

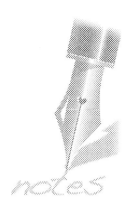

notes

3

The Inner Coach

A powerful force within you

We all receive constant information from outside sources. We may be getting suggestions from peers, staff, customers, competition, analysts, or even the media. Our boss should be our most important source of feedback, and it is always critical to understand that perspective, even if we don't agree.

However, it is also important to know the coach within. All of us have a presence inside that gives direction and guidance. Some call this intuition or a "gut" feeling. We call this the voice of the "inner coach." This is the supportive, honest inner force that will not allow you to make excuses, rationalize, or constantly blame others. A healthy inner coach helps you to forgive yourself for the times you may have fallen short and always has your best interest at heart.

PRACTICE

Think of a decision or a change you must make. Draw a chart with two columns labeled *Head* and *Heart.*

In the column entitled *Head,* write down reasoned or analytical solutions to the issue. What do you think should be done? What is the smart or rational approach? What does the information you have gathered suggest that you do?

In the *Heart* column, let your emotions guide you to a potential resolution. What do you feel you should do? Let your intuition inform you about the issue. Ask yourself why you feel so passionate.

The two voices of our inner coach can direct us to take the best course of action. Develop these very different perspectives. They can become wise personal advisors and powerful sources of inspiration.

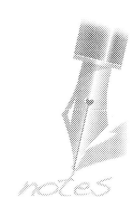

4

The Discipline of Practice

Repetition is Powerful

Most people don't have the luxury for practice time on the job like athletes, musicians, artists and performers. Yet we know that, if we want to improve or develop a new skill, we need to put in extra practice time. The more we practice with dedication and focus, the more quickly we improve.

What skills should be developed to improve your performance? Maybe you need to get better at setting expectations or giving and receiving feedback. Perhaps you want to write more clearly, communicate better, or have more courage to make difficult decisions.

Whatever your challenge, remember that repetition is king. Do more "reps" than is required and you will develop greater confidence and improve faster.

PRACTICE

Before an upcoming meeting where well-developed communication skills are required, choose one that you want to improve. For example, do you need to talk less or find the courage to speak up? Can you make your point with greater influence and fewer words? Do you communicate to others with your presence? An effective connection is not only about what is heard, but also what is felt.

Go to the meeting with the motivation to communicate clearly. Practice in advance alone or with a colleague until it feels less mechanical and more natural. You may even want to record your rehearsal for instant feedback. Check with others to see if this new routine is working. It may take some time to break old patterns, but the result will be worth it.

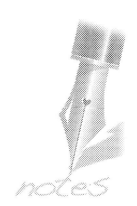

notes

5

The Art of Listening

Seek to understand

Your future success may be dependent on your ability to listen. The best leaders have developed into outstanding, active listeners.

Communication is not simply exchanging information, but rather connecting with another person and understanding his or her point of view. A great listener creates an awareness that the other person feels heard and valued. They find that others become more willing to share things with them, which allows important issues to surface.

Making others feel heard is critical for relationships. Listening is a powerful tool in negotiation, and an essential skill for leaders. Great listeners have a powerful receptive presence and an authentic desire to understand another point of view or idea.

PRACTICE

Are you a good listener? Here are a few questions to consider:

- Do you find yourself formulating your next point while others are speaking?

- Do other people ever tell you that you are a good listener?

- Who is the best listener you know?

To become a better listener, be fully present, ask questions that show you care, avoid interruptions, and re-state the message in your own words.

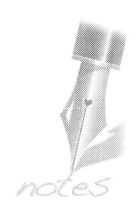

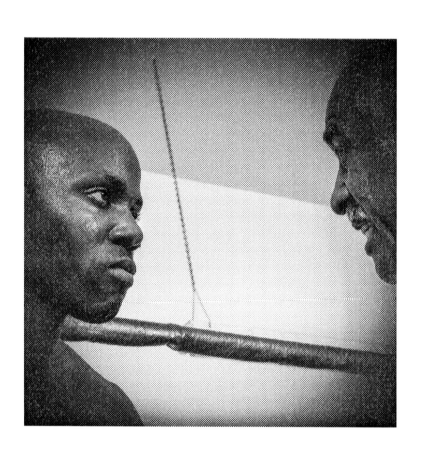

6

The Gift of Feedback

Another point of view

Feedback can be the important information you ask for to improve. When you feel that something is not going well, or you want a different perspective, observations and suggestions from someone you trust can help. There is no sense in ignoring your concerns or thinking that a problem will just go away. Even the people closest to you may be unaware of the issues you face. Perhaps they know something that needs to be addressed, but are uncomfortable talking to you about it.

Accepting what is said without defensiveness can be difficult. When you are open and willing to listen without attacking the messenger, others will be more willing to tell you the truth.

Giving and receiving feedback requires courage; it is one of the most underutilized tools in business. Feedback should always be considered a gift.

PRACTICE

It is important to ask for help or feedback from the right people. Identify individuals who have your best interest at heart. Schedule some time to meet with them privately. You might even choose a location out of the office. Tell your co-worker or boss that you are looking for honest and direct feedback and want to hear their perspective. Listen carefully, take notes, and ask questions that demonstrate your genuine interest in their opinion.

No matter how difficult it may be to hear, thank them for their perspective. Your co-workers will be more willing to share vital information with you in the future if you demonstrate a genuine appreciation for their feedback.

7

The Value of Clear Expectations

Know what is needed

Setting clear expectations is an essential skill for teams to get a job done and to establish priorities. The more explicit you are about expectations, the better chance you will have to create more effective communication, trust, and mutual support.

Setting priorities usually involves a conversation and some give-and-take. Even if it is uncomfortable, dig a little deeper to make sure that everyone is aligned. This will prevent unnecessary ambiguity and miscommunication. Taking extra time to set clear expectations is always worth the investment.

PRACTICE

Set aside a few minutes at the end of meetings and ask the people on your team if they are clear about what is expected and needed. You may be on the same page or may have to agree-to-disagree. At least you will be clear about where everybody stands.

Do you have clear expectations about everyone showing up on time, how quickly we should respond to each other, or if we are in agreement about e-mailing or texting in meetings? These seemingly simple issues need to be discussed from time to time.

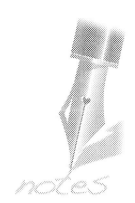

Section 2
Attitude

An authentic positive attitude is contagious. It's like a magnet that attracts others to want to work with you. A positive attitude has been proven through scientific study to have a profound effect on those around us.

A positive person communicates enthusiasm and optimism. Passion, commitment, and confidence, spontaneously show. A desire to improve and succeed demonstrates a competitive spirit.

Therefore, these following chapters are designed to help you develop an even more dynamic personality in the workplace.

8

A Burning Desire

Intensity comes from within

Aburning desire may be the most important quality you can have to be successful. It's an intensity that comes from within. Desire gives you the energy to focus and commit to your work. It is an inner drive pushing you to keep learning new things. It is the motivation to practice the skills that are essential for your success and to change what's not working. You really cannot have too much desire.

This passion pushes you to discover how good you can be. Your path to success can be encouraged by others but cannot come from them. A burning desire can only come from within you.

PRACTICE

Get a half dozen 3 by 5 cards. On each card, write down one thing you really want to accomplish. Keep it positive and very simple, using only a few words to say what you really want. Make sure it is something that is realistic and attainable.

Put one card in a place where you will see it every day. Continue placing the other cards in private places where you will see them often. These cards will serve as daily reminders to focus on your goal and the actions you must take to reach it.

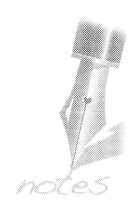

notes

9

Loving the Work

Enjoy what you do

You are very fortunate if your work gives you deep satisfaction and brings joy to your life. Possibly you work for a cause that is inspirational and expresses your values. Maybe it's a profession that is exciting and challenges your competitive nature or supports your intellect.

We all know that certain aspects of any job are not fun and can be boring. There may be days when the routine gets tedious. Pressure with your boss or co-workers can lead to burnout. Personal issues can be distracting.

If this happens to you, try not to focus on the negative and let it dominate your thinking. Remember why you chose your line of work and what about it you still really love. Focus on your strengths and the positive qualities you possess that have brought to where you are.

PRACTICE

Reflect on a time in your life when you really loved some endeavor. Perhaps it was playing on a sports team, singing in a band or choir, building something, working on a hobby, creating art, working in nature or volunteering. You did it because you loved it.

It's likely that you don't have that feeling about all aspects of your current work. However, reflect deeply about the aspects of your work that do inspire joy within you. Since most people are happier and perform better when doing something they truly love, discipline yourself to look for all the parts of your work that you enjoy and that make you happy.

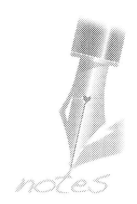

notes

10

Driving to Improve

At the top of your game

Actions in and out of the office show how much you care about improvement. Here are a few important questions to think about:

- Do I give full attention to my job?

- Do I make no excuses about the past?

- Do I welcome feedback from those I trust?

- Do I demonstrate mental toughness?

- Do I put in extra time?

While top performers generally want to be in roles that play to their strengths, they also have the willingness and courage to work on the areas where they want to improve. This is not an admission of weakness, but rather a demonstration of confidence and a desire for mastery.

PRACTICE

When you really want to work on improving anything, stop saying, "I have to" and start saying, "I want to."

Think and say:

- "I *want* feedback; it helps me improve."
- "I *want* to get better at dealing with conflict."
- "I *want* to challenge myself to be my best."

Now, <u>that's</u> a *Winning Spirit* attitude!

11

Competing With the Best

Dig deep inside

It is a good feeling to compete against individuals or companies that have outstanding skills and talent. This kind of competition can show you how good you really are. These opponents can become some of your most valuable teachers.

Who are your toughest competitors? Possibly they are colleagues who will compete with you for the next job or competitors who may battle with you in the marketplace.

Whoever you identify, develop a feeling of respect for your competition. If they have advantages, try not to be intimidated by them. Rather, appreciate that their proven success and desire to win helps you to become a more resilient and competitive performer. When you face a worthy competitor, you will be challenged to dig deep inside.

PRACTICE

Write about the following questions in your journal:

• Who are my toughest competitors?

• What makes them so tough?

• What can I learn from them?

• What positive attributes do I see in them that I also see in myself?

• Would they have me on their list of worthy competitors?

notes

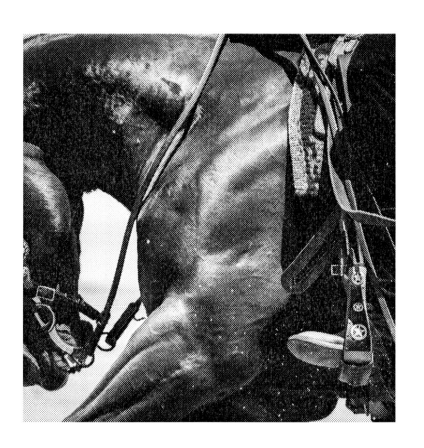

12

Breaking a Sweat

No substitute for hard work

If success in business came easily, without tremendous dedication and effort, it wouldn't mean as much and not be as sweet.

When you want to be outstanding and gain recognition in your field, hard work is not only necessary; it is something you do with tremendous passion and pride. Your desire to excel and your strong work ethic make you stand out and will earn respect from everyone.

Intensely focusing your effort not only improves your chances of achieving outstanding results but also improves your skills and makes everyone around you better. Most importantly, it gives you a sense of deep personal satisfaction.

PRACTICE

Look around your company and see who is *effectively* working. Notice those who are the most focused. They efficiently execute tasks and do not waste time complaining about things they cannot control. They make time for others, stay connected, and communicate clearly.

Make a list of hard workers you admire.

- Why did you choose them?

- How do they stand out?

- Would others choose you as a hard worker?

- Why would they do so?

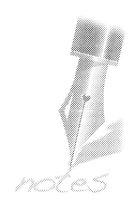

13

Having Some Fun

The kid within you

The pressures of your job can easily squeeze the joy out of your work. You can tire from extra effort, long hours or difficult travel. Situations may emotionally drain you. Demanding projects or financial pressure can temporarily beat down even the best performers. It is difficult to be an inspiring teammate or leader when one is feeling overwhelmed.

It is precisely at those times of acute stress, when a little fun would be a big help. Playfulness, even in small doses, is essential to sustaining your motivation.

Good leaders know when to exert pressure on their teams and when to relieve it. Having some fun will revive your spirit as well as your team. Lightheartedness is an important quality in the development of a *winning spirit.*

PRACTICE

Find something new to do with work colleagues that is both fun, inspiring, and within the acceptable norms of your company's culture. Frequently, colleagues go out for lunch or dinner, have coffee or a drink, go to an event, or play a game like golf or tennis. That type of out-of-the-office time can create good rapport, trust, and connection.

Now and then, escape the norms of everyday business. If you are athletic, shoot some baskets, meet for a workout or yoga, perhaps sneak away for a trip to the batting cage. If nature inspires you, take a walk in a beautiful place. Spend some time with an expert who is passionate about a field you enjoy. Cook with a chef, paint with an artist, play music or sing with a musician. You can also do something that is meaningful for others less fortunate. Think outside the cubicle.

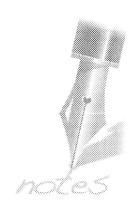

14

Testing Your Comfort Zone

Explore unfamiliar places

There are some days when efficient work comes easily. You can engage with intensity, focus, and energy. You and your co-workers come together into a flow, and the work seems to move without distraction. You deliver with confidence, creativity, and control. You are working in an area that is your *sweet spot*, your "zone."

However, no one always works in the zone. There will be days when it is difficult to find enough energy to make things happen, or when getting the results you expect from others feels out of your control.

On days when you are not performing at the top of your game, you will need to apply extra effort, concentration, and will power. Manufacturing energy and pushing yourself when you "don't feel like it," is the sign of a true pro.

PRACTICE

When you face a really tough situation, acknowledge the difficulty but don't dwell on the downside; this challenge will take extra energy and focus. Break it down into approachable steps. Dig in, do your best, and make it happen.

Perhaps you will need to improve a skill or develop more confidence to accomplish this task. Whatever your issue, find small ways to push yourself and get outside your comfort zone.

Develop the ability to call upon on your inner reservoir, especially when you need that extra energy to deal with difficult pressure situations.

notes

15

Walking Like a Champ

Executive Presence

Although bragging about accomplishments is not admirable, you should be proud of your success. If you're really good, there is nothing wrong with owning it. Being successful, you have become confident in your abilities, tough in pressure situations, and an effective leader.

When you are feeling good about your ability to perform at a high level, there is no need to hide it. You can project a quiet confidence and walk into any meeting or situation, knowing that you belong and can hold your own.

Find your natural sweet spot and others will sense your strong presence. When you've "got game," it's natural to be proud and feel like a champ. You've earned it.

PRACTICE

Visualize yourself walking into a meeting with a confident presence. Imagine that you're feeling good about your knowledge, skills, and preparation. This is how you project the essence of a champion.

By practicing this, you will become more comfortable in your own skin, moving with poise—centered and balanced.

Ask yourself these questions:

• Would you hire yourself?

• What do you think "quiet confidence" means?

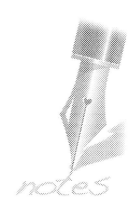

16

Never Giving Up

Fight for your dream

When you ask successful people about the key to their success, they often talk about the power of determination and will. They understand the absolute importance of having an unwavering commitment and never giving up. They know that persistent leaders rise to the top.

Looking back over your own life, you will see that some of your greatest achievements came as a result of your tremendous energy and persistence. Somehow, you knew you had the power to conquer the challenge you were facing, and you did! Having overcome a situation once, you know that you can do it again. So, when life gets tough, as it often does, dig deep and find that determined spirit within you. With steadfast conviction, believe with all your mind, heart, and gut that you can make it. This kind of attitude will help you through those tough times. No matter how difficult the challenge, fight for your dream!

PRACTICE

Recall a time in your life when you faced a huge challenge. Possibly the odds of success seemed to be against you and others around you didn't believe you could succeed. However, within you was a fierce power of determination and will. You knew that you could do it, and you did!

- What was the biggest challenge you've faced?

- How did you tap into yourself to overcome it?

notes

17

Balancing Your Life

Being well-rounded

While you may feel pressure to devote much of your attention to work, it's important not to let your job totally define your sense of self-worth. Your life includes so many other potential areas of interest; your profession is only a part of a full, rich life.

As you develop as a professional, recognize that some of your essential "to-dos" may be with your family and friends. These non work-related experiences can provide energy, perspective, and inspiration to look at business challenges differently.

Being a well-rounded person, you are more capable of enjoyment and success both in and outside of work.

PRACTICE

Ask your family members and good friends outside of work what they like and appreciate about you the most. Ask them what they think your best qualities are. Do not be surprised if they don't even talk about your job. Did anyone say anything that surprised you?

Now, ask a few trusted work colleagues the same question. It will be interesting to hear what positive qualities are similar and which are different from the ones you heard from family and friends.

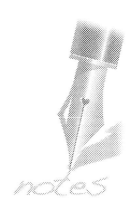

18
Creating a Winning Spirit
Positive Mental Attitude

Throughout a career, most professionals will have many different jobs and roles. Each is a new opportunity to develop greater self-mastery. A true winning spirit transcends bottom-line success or failure. Having a winning spirit is about developing an attitude of confidence: giving your best effort, working with heart and integrity, and making no excuses. By creating a winning attitude, you can stay focused, make those around you better, and never give up until the results are determined.

Take responsibility for what you can control and let go of the rest. Mentors, peers, subordinates, and even competitors will respect your professional attitude. Act and engage with honor and integrity in victory or in loss. That's a *winning spirit!*

PRACTICE

Think back to your most recent loss or setback and reflect on the following:

- Are you proud of your effort in that situation?

- Is there anything you would have changed?

Now, think about a recent win you have had:

- How did you handle your victory and success?

- What would others say about it?

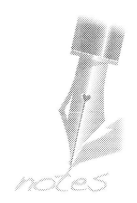

Section 3

The Mental Edge

Business success demands physical and mental excellence. Maintaining your physical health and understanding your mental edge are essential for top performance.

We frequently say that the "soft stuff is the hard stuff." The mental edge or inner game which has direct impact on performance can be developed by practicing specific skills. The ideas and PRACTICEs in this section are derived from sport psychology principles that we have applied to business.

The mental game is not reserved for elite performers. In the competitive world of business, learning these skills will help you perform at higher levels and everyone will have more fun in the process.

19

Feel the Flow

A sense of freedom

Creativity is not reserved only for professions focused on design, artistry, and imagination. Creativity happens when you work with a sense of freedom and can feel the flow, expressing your own unique style.

Creativity is the blending of your skill, intuition, and intelligence. While still having good fundamentals, you work fearlessly, but with discipline and control. As your creative mind engages with the project, you find yourself immersed in the moment. In these moments, you are completely present and time may feel like it is moving in slow motion.

Working creatively does not necessarily mean being fancy. Rather, it means that you have the freedom to be yourself and to get the job done your way. Then your work becomes art, as well as business.

PRACTICE

Go to a place where you enjoy just sitting and relaxing. It could be a park bench, your favorite coffee shop or somewhere in your home. Bring a journal that feels good to write in and a good quality pen. After you have settled in, think about someone to whom you would like to write an old fashioned letter.

This will be a rough draft letter, written with ease and without editing. It will simply be a stream of consciousness (flow) that you release from your hand to the paper. As you write your thoughts, get in touch with your emotions and put feeling into your letter. Let the pen move effortlessly and allow your ideas to manifest into written words.

It is important to not critique your letter; there will be time for that later. For now, don't worry about spelling or grammar. Just get into the writing process and feel the pleasure of expressing yourself on paper.

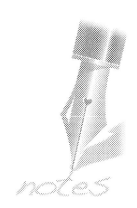

20

A Focused Mind

Finding intuitive solutions

Harnessing mental power is essential in achieving our goal. Mental practice can free us from distractions and help us create solutions to issues in ways we cannot yet imagine.

If we are willing to spend the time and have the discipline, we can train ourselves to access untapped states of mind. Top-level athletes often talk about being so immersed in the present moment that they play at a higher level. Other people from various backgrounds and disciplines have developed the ability to imagine solutions to issues that they cannot solve with rational thought. They have found ways to connect with their intuition.

As in sports, success in business also depends on finding intuitive solutions.

PRACTICE

There are many exercises to help you access more of your remarkable mental potential. Some practices help increase your ability to focus and concentrate under pressure. Some are designed to bring you more fully into the present moment. You can improve concentration can by focusing on your breath or on a sound. Quieting your mind allows intuitive solutions to surface. You will be amazed by how you generate ideas in bold new ways.

To start: find a place where you can be undisturbed. Get into a comfortable position, sitting in a chair with your hands folded in your lap. Keeping your back straight and your feet firmly on the floor, relax your shoulders and close your eyes. As you settle in, watch your breathing. Allow your breath to become full and deep and notice the air moving in and out. When thoughts pop into your head, guide your attention back to your breathing. This simple practice offers many benefits to your health and performance.

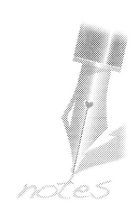

21

Inner Confidence

You can do it!

Sometimes you may feel that others are disappointed because you are not living up to their expectations. You may think that they are overlooking your abilities or not giving you enough support and encouragement. There may be times when there is friction with your boss or co-workers.

There is no question that all professionals need others to have trust in them. However, when you are not getting a feeling of confidence from those around you, search for the kind that no one else can give you. Find the confidence that comes from within.

To have inner confidence, you must have trust in your, preparation, work ethic, and mental toughness. When you know that you have what it takes, you can do it!

PRACTICE

Write down every business skill that you possess and make a list of your strengths. This may not be easy for you because you may think talking about our strengths is bragging. Take a break from that perception, and list all your talents and skills.

As you look at your list, put a plus (+) next to everything that you feel confident about. If you feel extremely confident, put a double-plus (++). Do not ask for anybody else's opinion; this has to come directly from you.

If you are honest with yourself, all the plusses will show just how confident you are. Be proud of those plusses, and "own" them. When you find a skill that did not get a plus, don't lose heart. Instead, think of this as a challenge and an opportunity to improve. Eventually, you will add more plusses to your list.

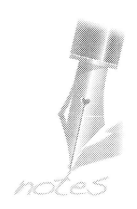

22

Positive Pressure

Thrive when the heat is on

Certain business environments are high-pressure and good leaders thrive in that environment. Professionals know they will have to channel the pressure they feel into poise and execution. Working under pressure is a big part of their jobs. They have likely chosen their careers because they find that intensity exhilarating.

If you are a competitive professional, this means that you have chosen to work under pressure and the critical eyes of others. You are a leader because you like making challenging decisions and have the freedom to take risks. This is a path you have chosen, and since pressure in your business world is unavoidable, why not accept it and let it help you perform even better? Use the pressure to bring out your intensity and competitive spirit. Say, "I love the pressure. Bring it on!"

PRACTICE

The night before your next big event, sale, or presentation, go into a room where you can be alone. Get into a comfortable, relaxing position. Then, imagine yourself in the situation you will be facing. Thinking about your upcoming event may cause you to feel some anxiety. That's okay!

As the intensity within you begins to build, breathe into it. Continue to let the pressure grow. Excited and full of energy, visualize yourself performing exactly the way you want. Create a mental picture of your success.

Breathing deeply, welcome that intensity, knowing that it will make you a better performer tomorrow. Remind yourself, "I love the pressure! Bring it on!"

notes

23

Beginner's Mind

Reawaken your curiosity

When you first started your job, you were eager to learn as much as you could. Your mind was open and your enthusiasm was high. Being new, you wanted to improve every day. You were excited to learn. Yet, over time, things can change as you experience highs, lows, successes and failures.

Have you ever noticed that some people have lost their kid-like enthusiasm and forgotten how excited they once felt and why they loved their work? Possibly they have become so successful that they take their natural abilities and hard-earned skills for granted, and the passion starts to fade.

If you find this happening to you, remember why you fell in love with your work. Recall the enthusiasm you once felt. Reawaken your curiosity and think like a beginner again.

PRACTICE

Whenever you feel overwhelmed with pressure or are just taking it all too seriously, reconnect with the earliest memories of your professional career.

Find something that reminds you of times when you first started working. Maybe you have a photo, an award, an article of clothing, a business card, or a memento from a project.

Remember the excitement you had in your early years of work. Recall how much fun you had and the friends that you made. Remember what it felt like to be a rookie or a beginner. Re-awaken your joy.

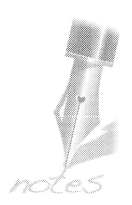

notes

24

Right Here, Right Now

Being in the Moment

Do you ever think that the next level is where the "big time" is? Don't be fooled. Never let your search for success in the future blind you to the treasures in the present. Right here is the best place for you, and right now is the best time.

It seems strange when you hear a leader talking about his past with a longing to somehow get it back. Although the past can teach us and the future can inspire us, neither are relevant in this moment.

Take a look around and see all that you have. Appreciate your job. Your work today is just as important as anyone else's. While it is good to have goals and aspire to higher levels, remember that the best place and time for you is now. Enjoy yourself and be glad to be where you are.

PRACTICE

Great performance only happens in the current moment. Each time you find yourself worrying about your future, wasting unnecessary energy by wondering what's going to happen, say to yourself, "Right here, right now."

Likewise, if you find yourself thinking about past mistakes and wishing that you could do it all over again, say to yourself, "right here, right now."

This simple, yet-powerful exercise, if practiced over and over, trains your mind to think in the present moment. Your attention focuses in the "here and now" and you get rid of useless thoughts about things that you can't control.

notes

25

Vivid Visualization

Imagine every possible detail

When you use your imagination, you can see things in your mind's eye before they manifest physically. You can see yourself making a big sale, finishing a project, or receiving a promotion.

Think about something you want to accomplish and visualize the necessary steps over and over in your mind's eye. As you daydream about every aspect of your goal, and see yourself achieving it, that image will create a huge level of confidence within you. The clearer your mental picture, the better your focus and results will be.

Before an important event or presentation, pretend that you are already there, performing the way you want. Rehearse every positive detail you can imagine. With your vivid imagination, visualize your desired success. When you see it in your mind, you will believe it in your heart and then can achieve it in the world.

PRACTICE

First, write down something that you want to achieve; a goal or dream that you really want to come true.

Next, create a mental picture of your goal. Add as much detail into this picture as possible. Visualize the people surrounding you and what you will be wearing. Imagine the sounds, smells and temperature as you paint a mental picture of the entire environment.

Finally, close your eyes and pretend that this very goal does come true. Let your imagination run wild and experience your success happening.

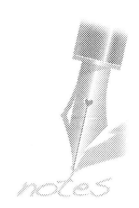

notes

26

Positive Words

Optimism works

Saying positive words can help turn your dreams into a reality. These are called affirmations, inspirational words or phrases that you say to yourself to help you remember your goal and focus on what you want to achieve.

When you say an affirmation, remember to keep it simple and speak to yourself in a natural way, as if you have already reached your goal. Set goals you feel are possible to reach, but don't limit yourself. It's good to set high standards and expect greatness. Think big! Say your words with feeling, meaning and conviction.

Think of these words as seeds being planted in your mind. With repetition, these words will firmly take root and help you to achieve your goal.

PRACTICE

Imagine that your boss or a peer who you really respect comes up to you and tells you something very positive about yourself. Their compliments and encouraging words fill you with confidence.

- What did that person say?

- What qualities and skills impressed them?

- What are the most powerful words you can say to yourself?

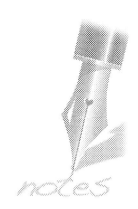

27

Recharge

Time to relax

Many of us live fast-paced lives, racing from activity to activity. We want to excel at work and still have time for our families and other interests. All too often, we feel the anxiety and pressure of falling behind. Even though finding time to relax may not seem to fit into our busy schedule, it is so important for our health, creativity and relationships.

There are many ways for you to recharge. You can listen to music, soak in hot water, take a walk or a nap. Even five minutes of meditation can begin to rejuvenate you. Stretching and conscious breathing help calm your nervous system and quiet your mind. Deep relaxation causes stress to fade as revitalizing energy flows through you.

Practice

If stress is being caused by an upcoming event or deadline, here is an easy, relaxing breathing exercise that can be done within minutes. Try to do this outside if possible, because natural light can have an immediate calming influence on your brain.

With your mouth closed, inhale to a count of four. Hold your breath to a count of four. Then with your mouth open, exhale to a count of eight.

Repeat this breathing pattern three-to-five times or until you feel the natural relaxing effect within your entire body.

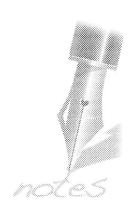

28

E + E = P

Emotion + Energy = Performance

Emotion + Energy = Performance is a formula we use in our work. Emotions are powerful and generate energy, and we think it's important to understand which emotions energize and which ones drain. Emotions affect people in unique ways. For many, positive emotions improve performance. For others, anger and fear motivate them to dig deeper and work harder. Some find that anger or fear shuts them down and they under-perform. For this reason alone, it's important to learn what emotions help you, and which ones set you back.

Showing emotion at work may not be acceptable. However, your emotions are real and, at the right time, it's okay to let them out. Sometimes you need to tell somebody how you feel. Emotions are part of life and letting your feelings out is essential for sustained success and happiness.

PRACTICE

"Mad, Sad, and Glad" is a powerful exercise in which you get to express a wide range of emotions.

Write down something involving work that has made you really mad. Next, write something that has made you feel sad. Finally, write something that makes you really glad.

• What emotions help you perform better?

• What emotions hurt your performance?

• What emotions influence your co-workers?

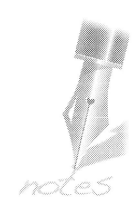

notes

Section 4

Connections

Connection to others is essential in almost every profession. Rarely is business a solo activity. Having a positive relationship with co-workers, clients, suppliers, employees, and bosses is important.

Connection is not just communication, an exchange of information Connection has to do with how you make people feel. It creates a link between two humans and can trigger powerful emotions.

If you are a leader, your connection to your staff will have an impact regarding their level of support, engagement and confidence. Inspiring leaders know that connection is crucial to bringing the best out of others.

29

Your Home Team

Those who support you

Who are people outside your work that you depend on? What roles do they play? They could be your spouse, partner, parents, children, friends, or anyone you rely on.

Some members of your home team may care for your children or help you with everyday needs. Some of these loyal teammates give comfort when you are down, sick, or hurt. They give advice when you need guidance and direction. They devote many hours of their time to you and your success.

Take a moment to realize how fortunate you are to have even one person that helps you in this way. Isn't it awesome that these people care so much about you? Go out of your way to thank them for all their time and energy. Tell them how much you love them. Appreciate your home team; they are a huge part of your success.

PRACTICE

Make a list of every member of your home team, and what you appreciate about them. Write them a note or an email, telling them how much you appreciate what they are doing for you. Your words and thoughtfulness will show them that all of their effort is worth it. Don't hold back. Be sure they know how thankful you really are. They will not only treasure your notes, but writing them will make you feel good, too!

If you are a business leader, you might encourage your staff to do this practice. You might even send a brief note of thanks to the spouse of someone on your staff that has put in extra hours taking them away from home. It is always reassuring to receive such a sincere and considerate message.

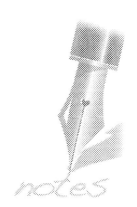

notes

30

Your Inner Circle

People who have your back

As a business professional you work in a competitive world. You will face tough opponents and situations. You will be evaluated at each level. Others will form opinions about you and comment on your talent, ability, and skill to perform under pressure. They will talk about you; sometimes they'll say good things, sometimes bad.

It is natural for you to care about what others think. But the only opinions that really matter are those from people who have your best interest at heart: your inner circle: mentors, trusted peers, coaches, family members, and true friends.

If you hear negative things it can be very tough to let go of these comments. Nevertheless, try not to put value in the opinions of people who don't have your best interest at heart. Letting go will make a big difference in how you feel about yourself.

PRACTICE

On a sheet of paper, draw a large circle. Then write the initials of the people who really care about you and have your best interest at heart. Place them at different locations within the circle; you may want to place the ones you currently rely on the most, closest to the center.

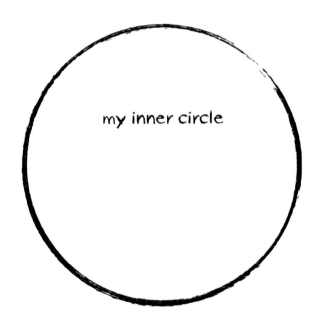

my inner circle

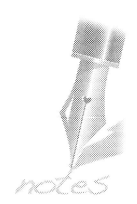

31

Essential Conversations

Words are powerful

From time to time we all struggle with the people that are essential to our success. Connecting and communicating with them is important, especially if the issue is holding you back. To move forward, you will want to engage in a conversation to clarify things and resolve your differences.

Finding the courage to talk to such a person isn't always easy. It can be difficult to raise an issue because you may think that you will be rejected. Possibly this person may have information that cannot be shared with you and will not be able to give you a direct answer.

When you meet, explain things in a way that is easy to understand, using simple and direct words. When your message is clear, there is no confusion about what is expected and a new level of trust can be built.

PRACTICE

The next time you feel concerned or confused about something that involves your boss or anyone else, for that matter, ask for some time when you can sit down and talk privately about what is on your mind. You may want to write down your thoughts before the meeting so that you will remember everything you want to say.

Be specific and demonstrate a willingness to listen as well as to talk. Don't assume that this person knows what you are thinking or understands what you are feeling. By asking truthful questions, you will develop trust and learn more about the other person's perspective.

If you do this whenever it is needed, your relationships will improve and you will find it easier to communicate in the future.

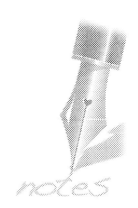

notes

32

Courageous Dialog

Honesty takes courage

There may be situations at work that are difficult to deal with. Often the difficulty comes from a lack of communication or a misunderstanding. If the problem is with a boss, employee, or colleague, dysfunctional relationships of this type reflect badly on both parties, no matter who is right or wrong. You will want to work through the conflict by confronting the situation with the other person. When you clear the air, you can focus on the real work that needs to be done.

Sometimes it is tough to bring up sensitive issues, but you must be willing to talk. Have courage and take time to work things out. Find a place where you can be alone and can talk face-to-face. Get your feelings off your chest. Be as direct and honest as possible. Try to get to the heart of the matter. Listen well and be ready to hear what the other person has to say.

PRACTICE

Observe how people you know deal with difficult situations. You may find that many people say they are going to clear the air with someone, but when it comes down to it, they can't find the courage to discuss their disagreements, frustrations, or challenges.

Learning to have courageous dialog is an advanced practice. It takes superior listening skills and wisdom. It may require you to forgive others or yourself. Because you will be dealing with emotionally charged issues, you will have to show some compassion and empathy.

When you find people who are brave enough to confront tough situations head-on, ask them how they do it. Ask them how they find the courage to not back down and have the strength to work things out. What situation or person in your life is difficult to deal with?

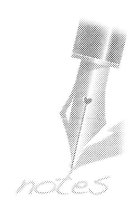

33

Compassion

Treat others with respect

In competitive business, compassion is not often talked about. In your professional life, you may not be able to put yourself in someone else's shoes. It could be seen as a sign of weakness. You may be conditioned to think mainly about your own team, resources, and personal success.

However, you can be a competitive professional and still be a compassionate person. You can treat others the same way you would like to be treated. You can be gracious when you are successful, and be empathetic for others that are not.

Also, when you have compassion, you care about more than just your own success. Although you may excel at what you do, in the big scheme, no one is more important than anyone else. You look for the good in people and you radiate kindness and humility, qualities that are at the heart of true champions.

PRACTICE

Compassion requires you to see and feel an issue through someone else's perspective. Being empathetic requires understanding a point of view that is not your own and an emotion that you do not feel.

When you see others having a tough time, this is an opportunity to practice a little compassion. From your own experience, you know that there are many things that can cause people to feel down: a tough decision, loss of a job or resources, unexpected change, getting sideways with your boss, or a personal problem.

The best thing you can do is to simply ask if they are okay and if there is anything you can do to help. Be a superior listener. Take a few moments, and try to see the issue fully from their perspective. You don't have to give advice or offer solutions. Just let them tell you what they are thinking and feeling. Walk in their shoes and show that you care. Sometimes that's all it takes.

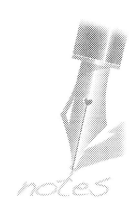

Section 5

Comeback

If you are a business professional, you have likely found yourself in a situation where you have failed. Everyone who pushes the edge will find themselves suffering a loss at some point in their career.

It's not a question of "if, but rather "when." Perhaps you have been willing to take on a high-risk role, or been promoted into a job for which you are not ready. How you react when things do not go your way is a true test of your competitive spirit.

There is nothing sweeter than come-from-behind success.

34

Fear as an Advantage

Every competitor deals with fear

Fear is a very powerful emotion that may protect us from taking unnecessary risks. At the same time, deep-seated fears may hold us back and stifle our career. If your fear is holding you back, how will you deal with it?

Some are physical, others financial. There's the fear of losing your job, making mistakes, being criticized, and feeling exposed. Facing them is a huge advantage because our fears can rob us of confidence, causing us to over-think and tighten up.

Sometimes the thing you fear will occur, the loss will be difficult and you will need to radically accept what has happened. As you pay close attention to the situation, ask yourself, "Why am I afraid?" By doing this, you begin to let go and use fear to your advantage.

PRACTICE

If you ever find yourself having a fear that is affecting your energy or performance, find a place where you can be alone for 5 to 10 minutes. Then, imagine that the very thing that you fear does happen. Bring what you fear most out in the open. When you do so, you gain power over it. No matter what happens, you will still have yourself, your strengths and talents, your core confidence, your true friends, and your passion for success.

Now imagine success. This time, see everything happening just the way you want. Visualize the outcome you desire.

- What is the advantage of facing your fear?

- After facing your fear, why is it important to go back and visualize a positive outcome?

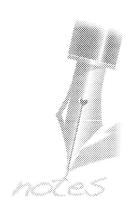

35

Learn from Failure

Fail fast and move on

Business has its risks. If you work long enough, you will not escape being humbled or embarrassed by making mistakes in front of others. You could lose your courage or ability to perform in the clutch.

When you have a failure, let your disappointment be the fuel that gives you even more motivation. Think about the things you want to change and the lessons you have learned from your loss.

It is normal to feel the pain of loss and the frustration of failure, but don't dwell on it too long. When you suffer a setback or make a critical mistake, take the time to learn from it and put it behind you. Fail fast and move on.

PRACTICE

Think about the biggest mistake or disappointment you have experienced. It could have to do with losing a big client, not executing under pressure, or being passed over for a promotion. You may have even lost your job.

- What lesson did you learn?

- What will you do differently next time?

- How does losing give you greater motivation?

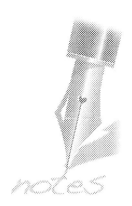

notes

36

Protect Yourself

There's only one you

In the world of business, there are going to be times when you need to protect yourself. Your confidence may be attacked, intentionally or unintentionally. Someone could be jealous of you, be competing with your job or resources and may attempt to undermine you. Your boss or the company may have placed you in a no-win situation. This is a time for self-protection.

Although your feelings may be shaken, nobody can rob you of your confidence; it is based on trusting your hard-earned skills and talents. Unless you allow it, nobody can steal the belief in yourself. Self-worth does not depend on what others say or think.

Also, as a hardworking professional, you naturally become fatigued now and then. You have to know when to push through and when to rest and recharge. Protect yourself by being mindful of your health and safety. There is only one you!

PRACTICE

Good preparation is the first line of defense. Becoming aware of your nutrition, fitness, and sleep habits will improve your game. As you know, there is no magic formula; everyone has his or her own zone for peak performance.

In your journal, write down the foods, fitness, and amount of sleep you need to keep you in the zone. Craft a peak performance plan that is realistic and easily followed. You might start with how much sleep you need each night, how many workouts you need each week, and a very basic plan to improve your nutrition a little every day.

The important point is that you understand what it takes to feel really good and have the energy to perform at the top of your game.

Section 6

Post Game

You will have big moments in your career, moments when significant events happen. What do you do after those moments?

Do you take time to celebrate your success? What are you giving back? How are you showing gratitude to those who have helped you? These "post game reflections" should not be saved for your retirement, but rather integrated into the small, noticeable moments that happen along the way. Learning to be fulfilled while you are working is an important part of success. It will help keep you in the flow of the present moment, and give more meaning to your job.

37

Celebrate Success

Enjoy what you've done

It feels good when you personally succeed and your company or team wins. It feels even better when you reach a goal that you have been striving for. When you stop and think about the time, effort, and dedication that you have put into that success, it's impressive.

Your good fortune has not come easily. The team and personal success you experience is a statement about you, about the commitment you made and what you have given up. Your success is not the result of what happened in a single moment, but rather the accumulation of weeks, months, or years of preparation and hard work.

Take time to enjoy your accomplishments and celebrate your success. Be proud of what you have earned and enjoy it while it lasts. Give your teammates and yourself some time to savor the win before jumping back in. You all deserve it.

PRACTICE

Sometimes in business, an ultimate success can take a long time to come into fruition. It can take years for some projects to be completed. Therefore, it is important to acknowledge little wins.

Celebration does not always mean having a party. Researchers at the University of California at Berkeley analyzed a season of NBA game film. Winning teams acknowledged each other more on the little things like a good shot, pass, screen, or defensive play. These "touch points" of small celebration might be a hand slap, fist bump, touched forearm, a pointed finger, or an eye-to-eye-connection. Winning leaders know the importance of creating rituals that celebrate success.

Identify those little things that you and your team do that truly make a difference. Create your own mottos, rituals and gestures that acknowledge when you have done a good job. Teammates will be inspired to do more when you celebrate. Enjoy the journey of both big and small accomplishments along the way.

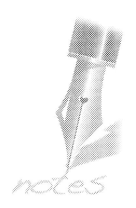

notes

38

Giving Back

Help others

No matter what your age, if you have been a serious professional for a while, you have most likely gained valuable knowledge about your business. You understand the meaning of desire and dedication. You have developed sound skills, strong work habits, and the ability to focus.

To continue growing as a person, it is important that you give back to others. There will always be less experienced professionals and others who will want to know what you know and be able to do what you do.

At the right time and place and in a friendly and caring way, give back some of the same positive energy, knowledge, and enthusiasm that was given to you. It is often said that the best way to master something is to teach it to others. When you do this, you are completing a cycle of giving and receiving. Helping others helps us.

PRACTICE

Think of yourself as a coach or mentor, not a boss or supervisor, to someone who would benefit from your help, skills or advice. Your job is to help bring the best out of them and not do the work for them. Maybe your role is to help them identify and acquire new skills or build new relationships.

They may need encouragement or advice to work through a challenging situation. If appropriate, become a trusted sparring partner, challenging and pushing this person to be better, but doing so in a safe environment and without the desire to dominate.

Help them find and achieve their own goals, not the goals or dreams you may have for them. This is the same thing you would have wanted from a coach or mentor as you were coming along. Giving back will remind you of the basics that made you successful.

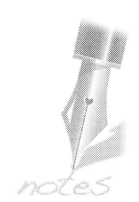

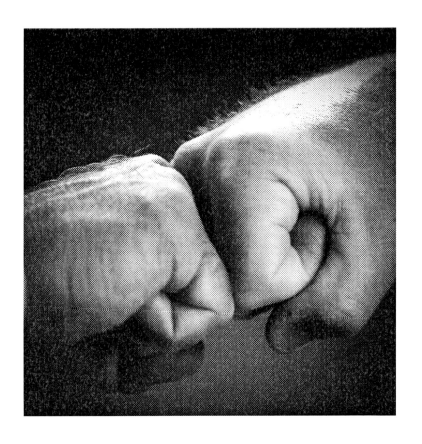

39

Honor the Game

Business is a noble endeavor

Business is a noble endeavor. It provides shelter, food, health and education for your family. It strengthens communities by providing important services and opportunities. Economic vitality and prosperity give youth hope for a better future. If you are a leader and have others working for you, think of how many families your business supports.

What is given always comes back to us and, over time, those who are honest, determined, and focused on delivering real value tend to be the long-term winners.

Striving to be your best in your job helps other parts of your life come into focus. It teaches important lessons and rewards you with memories and friendships that will last a lifetime.

PRACTICE

Imagine you were creating a dream team of performers for your company or department. You could choose anyone you have personally known or met. You could put each of them in any role you needed. They would demonstrate the essence of teamwork--considerate, unselfish and skilled. In your mind, you have created your "dream team." This team would work together in ways you have never seen before.

Imagine what you could accomplish and the positive energy that you all would create together. See how everyone would bring the best out of each other! Visualize the product or service you would produce and how that might change others lives.

This idealized state is the perfect team. While it may not be as you imagine, it does show you the power and potential of business teams to make a mark in the world

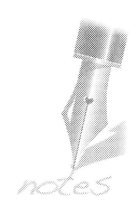

notes

40

Appreciate It All

Gratitude is powerful

Serious and dedicated professionals set high standards for themselves. It is extremely rewarding for them to see how far they can take their success. However, every now and then, it's not a bad idea to just appreciate what you have and how much you have already accomplished. Be grateful that you are part of the world of business and the thrill and intensity of competition it offers. Be thankful for the relationships you have built, and how the money you have made has provided for you. It is good to want more. Just make sure to take some time to appreciate what you already have.

Gratitude is a powerful force. Being grateful improves your state of mind and your relationships with others. Expressing genuine appreciation is the ultimate principle in developing your *Winning Spirit.*

PRACTICE

Before falling asleep, lie down and think about many of the good things that have come your way because of your work. Before you drift off, feel how incredibly fortunate you are.

Appreciate all that you have right now: all of your skills and knowledge; all of your accomplishments, both big and small; the pride you have felt when you did your job well; the good feeling when someone noticed your contribution; and the money you have earned to provide for your family.

Appreciate those that helped you achieve. They may be bosses, mentors, co-workers, educators, friends and family members. They may have helped you learn or grow, provided a role that you depended on, or had your back when you needed them. They may have even pushed you to get better when you didn't want to be pushed.

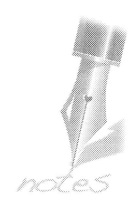

notes

Tom Mitchell

Tom's passion for exploring the boundaries of performance and leadership began as an athlete in his native Pennsylvania. His avid study of psychology, leadership, and personal development has led Tom to a richly varied career as a collegiate coach, professor, NBA team counselor, corporate executive coach, author and speaker.

Co-founder of MVP Performance Institute, Tom works closely with business leaders in a wide range of industries, focusing on team dynamics, leadership development and life transitions. His straightforward methods and practices reveal the importance of tapping into one's "inner game," which leads to greater team and individual performance.

Along with NFL legend Joe Montana, Tom co-authored *"The Winning Spirit, Sixteen Timeless Principles that Drive Performance Excellence"* [Random House 2005] and *"Winning Spirit Basketball"* [Skyhorse 2011] with Chris Mullin, NBA Hall of Famer.

Tom lives in the wine country of Northern California.

Hilleary Hoskinson

Hilleary Hoskinson is co-founder of *MVP Performance Institute,* a company focused on forming, aligning, and driving business teams to deliver outstanding results. Since 2004, he has brought MVP's unique performance edge to a broad range of companies, domestic and global, Fortune 500 to entrepreneurial. The MVP experience spans many industries including healthcare, construction, technology, telecommunications, consumer product, financial services, hospitality, and manufacturing.

Prior to his current position at MVP, he was a CMO, marketing, and product management executive at several technology and publishing companies. He was on the founding team and first General Manager of *Fast Company* magazine.

Hilleary is a cum laude graduate of Dartmouth College where he was the men's lacrosse captain, receiving both All-American and first team All-Ivy honors.

He lives in northern California.